Paddy and the Wolves

Paddy's mother sends him out
to the pastures because Paddy is fidgety at prayer.
Paddy is often fidgety at prayer,
but glad to help the Irish shepherd Barra
watch over the sheep.

Then Paddy wanders into the woods.

Paddy and the Wolves imagines
the world that the saint knew as a boy.
Patrick grew up in a place filled with
flashy fish and furry friends,
bears and bluebells,
delights and dangers
—all calls to prayer.

*Steve Nagel imagines how Patrick's character
and his later life of faith and courage might be tokened
in childhood adventures. Steve worked for many years
as the editorial and art director
at Saint Mary's Press in Minnesota.*

*Jen Norton creates a lush panorama of Paddy's world.
Jen is an award-winning contemporary Catholic folk artist.
She believes that through art,
"one can hear the whisper of a mighty Creator."*

To
Kathleen Buckley Nagel
and William Robinson Nagel
—*Steve*

I dedicate my work in this book
to my ever-supportive husband, Anthony, who has both literally
and figuratively made the pilgrimage with me up St. Patrick's
mountain (Croagh Patrick) in County Mayo, Ireland.
And to my daughter, Emma, who, like Paddy,
struggles with patience for prayer. Still, God is speaking
to her heart in the language she understands.
—*Jen*

Designed and built by Steve Nagel
Edited by Jerry Windley-Daoust
Copyedited by Nancee Adams-Taylor
Story consultation by Barbara Nagel
Copyright © 2016 by Steve Nagel
All rights reserved. No part of this book may be reproduced by any means
without the written permission of the publisher.
Printed in the United States of America
First Edition: 2016
ISBN 978-1-944008-30-7

Peanut Butter & Grace Books are published by Gracewatch Media,
Winona, Minnesota.
www.gracewatch.media
www.pbgrace.com

A Story About Saint Patrick When He Was a Boy

Paddy and the Wolves

Told by Steve Nagel and
Illustrated by Jen Norton

peanut butter & grace books

Gracewatch Media

Winona, Minnesota

"Paddy, you are too fidgety!"

Paddy was often scolded for fidgeting during prayer,
when he should be talking to God.

Paddy fidgeted again as his mother scolded him.
"When will you learn to be still during morning prayers?"

"I'm sorry, mother," Paddy said, and he truly meant it.
But his legs wanted to run!

"Put your fidgeting to good use, then," his mother said.
"Go help Barra. He is moving the sheep to the high pasture."

She gave Paddy some oatcakes to take with him
and blessed his bowed head.
"May Jesus go with you," she said.

Outside, Paddy flew up the path to find Barra,
munching a bit of an oatcake on the way.
He knew they must last the day.

The morning sun shone bright
on the springtime meadow and the woods.

Off in the distance, fishing boats moved slowly
across the silvery sea.

The big shepherd was always glad to see Paddy.
Barra, who came from Ireland across the sea,
greeted the boy with a big smile.

"Come to keep me company, young gentleman?" Barra asked.

Paddy was glad to keep company
with the friendly shepherd and his dogs.

Paddy was too young to guard the sheep.

Protecting them was a job for Barra and Lakon,
Ferox, and Issa.

Paddy did help Barra.
He warned Barra if he saw danger.
Paddy watched for sheep that strayed from the flock—
and he watched for wild animals that might hurt
straying sheep or carry off one of the lambs.

"If you help me move the sheep to the high pasture,"
Barra said, "then you may use my second-best staff,
if it is not too big for you."

"It's not too big!" Paddy said.

After Barra counted the sheep, he blew on his whistle—*tweet! teetee!*
twut!—and the dogs began herding
the flock up the hillside.

Barra followed the dogs,
and Paddy followed behind Barra.

Paddy's father said that Barra was a very good shepherd.
The sheep knew Barra's voice. They trusted him.

Barra took good care of the sheep,
and the sheep provided many good things
for Paddy's family: wool for warm clothing,
and milk and cheese and meat.

Paddy remembered his mother's scolding and thought:
Barra began praying with us, after he became a Christian.

Paddy liked listening to Barra's burry voice when he said prayers.

Tweet! Tweet!

Barra piped two sharp sounds on his whistle,
and the dogs began circling the sheep, bunching them together
and hurrying them away from some danger.

What was the danger? A wolf? Paddy thought.
No—it was a bear, a young bear, ambling over the hillside.

Sometimes bears were a danger to sheep.
Paddy stayed very still, waiting to see what the bear would do.

Barra moved between the flock and the bear,
standing tall with his stout shepherd's staff.

The bear barely looked at the shepherd.
It didn't want to hurt the sheep or fight with the dogs.

14

Instead the bear sauntered into a huge patch of shamrocks.

It began happily tearing up pawfuls of plants to eat.

Paddy knew that bears love shamrocks.
The bear would be busy all morning, stuffing itself.

Paddy raised his staff anyway.
I'll chase the bear away, he thought.

"Come, young gentleman," Barra called.
"Leave the bear be. The creature is being peaceful,
so we will leave it in peace. Let it tuck into its breakfast."

Twee, Twee, Tweet!
Barra whistled his dogs to guide the flock
along a path near the woods, and Paddy followed.
Barra was the shepherd and Paddy's friend and so Paddy obeyed.

Paddy came to a rocky stream flowing out of the woods.

He stopped at the bank and looked
into the clear water.

Speckled fish darted through the creek, too quick to be caught.

Paddy flopped on his stomach
and scooped up a handful of cold water.

Paddy thought,
Barra won't mind if I take a look into the woods.

The woods held dangers.
They were full of beauty as well.

Oaks taller than any building stood like kings.
Birds sang, unseen in the tops of the big trees.

Paddy wandered into the woods
and found wildflowers carpeting the forest floor—
orange poppies, red catchflies, and yellow primroses.

Jesus before me,
Jesus behind me,
Jesus beneath me,
Jesus above me.
Praise Him.

bluebells

20

Paddy walked on and then suddenly laughed.

In front of him was the best flower of all, the bluebells.

Here were more bluebells
than Paddy had ever seen in one place—
a big blue roadway, as wide as the road
that went though the town where Paddy's father worked.

Beauty seemed everywhere around Paddy.
He remembered the prayer from this morning.

Jesus before me,
Jesus behind me,
Jesus beneath me,
Jesus above me.
Praise him.

Paddy followed the bluebells farther into the woods.

It was darker and cooler. He pulled his cloak tighter.

In spots where the sunlight could reach the forest floor,
Paddy found blueberry plants.
He picked and nibbled berries as he walked.

Paddy bent down to pick a last handful of berries.

"Yikes!" A movement made him jump back.
A big snake was sunning itself on a sandy patch.

"Be gone, snake!" Paddy shouted, raising his staff.

The snake only gazed back at Paddy sleepily.

Paddy remembered Barra's words:
It's being peaceful, so we will leave it in peace.

Paddy walked on, away from the snake.

Paddy was well into the woods now. But he was not lost.
He began working his way downhill.
He knew that going downhill, he would come out of the woods
and find Barra and the dogs.

Paddy jumped down a rocky outcrop—
and into the middle of three wolf cubs playing together.

Paddy was delighted.

And then he saw the wolf den . . .

. . . and the mother wolf.

The mother wolf watched Paddy.

She growled, low and long.

Paddy could see her teeth.

Paddy clutched his shepherd's staff tighter.

It was heavy in his hands.
He knew in his heart that he could not wield the staff against a wolf.

He thought of his mother's blessing:
May Jesus go with you.

Paddy prayed. *Jesus, tell me what to do.*
Paddy prayed, and the wolf cubs began playing around him.
Paddy watched them prancing before him, behind him, all around him.

Jesus in the eyes of everyone around me.
Jesus in the ears of everyone around me.

That's it! thought Paddy, putting down his staff.

He got down on his hands and knees
and took an oatcake from his pocket.

Paddy prayed again.

Jesus in the mouths of everyone around me.

Paddy broke up the oatcake and scattered crumbs among the cubs.

The cubs sniffed at the crumbs
and snapped them up delightedly.

The mother wolf stopped showing her teeth.
She sat and watched quietly.

Paddy slowly picked up his staff.

He stepped away from the cubs.

The cubs wanted to follow Paddy, their new playmate.
The mother wolf barked a bit, and the cubs scurried back to her.

As Paddy moved away from the den,
he kept his eye on the wolves as long as he could.

Then he ran downhill.

Tweet! Tweet! Tweet!

Barra's whistle. Paddy knew it was meant for him.
Barra was looking for him. Paddy ran toward the sounds.

Coming out of the woods, he was met by Lakon, Ferox, and Issa.
They were happy to see him,
and greeted him with yipping and licking.

And Paddy was happy to see them and Barra.

Barra grinned, "The dogs were worried, Paddy,
and so we came looking for our lost sheep."

38

Paddy told Barra about the wolves.

Barra took a long look at Paddy.
"That was a wild wander you took this fine morning.
But it's well done, young gentleman, finding the wolves.
We will keep a watch on that patch of woods."

Barra's praise made Paddy happy.
He couldn't wait to get home to tell his mother how brave he was.

As the flock entered the lush grass of the high pasture,
Paddy said one more prayer:
Praise to you, Jesus. Thank you for your protection and care.

And thank you for flashy fish and furry friends!

Prayers of Saint Patrick, adapted for children

I wake up today with
Jesus before me,
Jesus behind me,
Jesus beneath me,
Jesus above me, and
Jesus with me all day long.

I begin today with
Jesus in the eyes of everyone around me,
Jesus in the ears of everyone around me,
Jesus in the mouths of everyone around me,
and Jesus in the hearts of everyone around me.

I thank God all day long for
the red fire,
the soft wind,
the green earth,
the deep sea,
the white clouds,
the tall mountains,
the blue sky,
the yellow sun,
the silver moon,
the bright stars, and
the loveliness of heaven.

A Prayer at Mealtime

We thank God for
bread and butter,
corn and carrots,
milk and meat,
cake and cookies.

We thank God for the family and friends
whom we share our supper with today.

Celebrate Saint Patrick's Day

* Get together with family and friends.
* Read the story of Paddy.
* Tell a bit about Patrick's adult life.
* Share some of the prayers.
* Cook up a supper with some green food.
* Serve oatcakes for dessert.
* Sing along to a Celtic song.
* Pick out a tune on a tin whistle.

Bake a batch of oatcakes

Ingredients
1/4 cup milk
1/4 cup sugar
1/4 tsp. baking powder
3/4 cup butter
2-1/2 cups rolled oats
1-1/4 cups flour
1/2 cup raisins
1/2 cup chopped walnuts (optional)

Instructions
Heat oven to 325°F/163°C.
Beat milk, sugar, baking powder, and butter until creamy.
Stir in oats, flour, and raisins.
On a floured surface, roll out the dough to 1/2 inch thickness.
Cut out 2-inch circles and place them on a greased cookie sheet.
Bake for 15 minutes until lightly golden.
Makes 40 cookies.
Keep in an airtight container until serving.
Optional: Decorate the cookies with icing stripes to create six segments.

Use the back cover artwork as a game

* Use it as a board game with dice; one will do. Let the kids make up rules for what happens when they land on a shamrock or an oatcake.

* Use it to tell the story: A child can point at the images and describe what happened.

Paddy and the Wolves is available as a coloring book at gracewatch.media.

Things You Might Not Know about Saint Patrick and Saint Patrick's Day

Patrick is the patron saint of Ireland and the missionary credited with converting Ireland to Christianity. Skip along to the shamrocks and the parades and that's maybe all most of us know. That's too bad. Patrick was a fascinating person, so here's some things worth learning about Patrick and about Saint Patrick's Day.

Patrick wrote an autobiographical sketch called the *Confession*.

It's brief, partly because Patrick felt he was not a writer, but it does tell us how he wants his life understood: "If what I have accomplished in life has been pleasing to God, in even a slight way, then let no one attribute this to me in my ignorance. On the contrary, let them be in no doubt that it was all simply due to the grace of God."

Patrick lived in a Christian and Roman world.

Patrick lived within the Roman Empire in the 400s A.D., during the time the Empire was failing—and may have already pulled out of Britain. The British Church remained connected to the Roman world: Patrick's father was a deacon and his grandfather, a priest. Patrick himself may have prepared for the priesthood in Brittany.

Patrick was a Briton by birth.

Probably Patrick was a Briton—one of the Gaelic-speaking people who lived in the west of Roman Britain. We know he had a Gaelic name at birth. Hamlets and farmsteads dotted western Britain as Patrick knew it. He says his upbringing was "simple and rustic."

Patrick was kidnapped by Irish raiders.

Patrick says, "When I was a rebellious sixteen-year-old, I was taken captive to Ireland along with many others." He was set to work shepherding. Even while he was a slave, Patrick's prayed, he says, night and day, and his faith grew. "It was there ...I turned with all my heart to the Lord my God...."

Patrick was Irish by affiliation.

After six years as a slave and shepherd, Patrick escaped by boat but returned home a changed person. He had a vision in which the voice of the Irish people called to him "'We beg you, holy boy, to come and walk again among us.'" Patrick left his family again and returned to Ireland to bring the Christian faith to its people. He persisted in his efforts for maybe forty years, and his mission met with all sorts of resistance. He was robbed, attacked, and imprisoned, but Patrick never gave up. He succeeded in converting thousands, he says—both chieftains and commoners. Before the Irish, no people had submitted to the Christian faith that were not within the Empire.

Patrick lived the Gospel, afflicting kings and comforting slaves.

Patrick detested slavery, in a way only a person who had been a slave might—at a time when maybe a quarter of the population of the Roman Empire were slaves. Slaves were considered merely another kind of property. In his *Confession*, Patrick pleads the plight of women slaves, saying that they faced special threats and terrors.

Patrick's staff had its own story.

Patrick is often portrayed holding a crozier. In tradition, the staff was given to Patrick by a hermit who had received it from Jesus himself. Legend has it that Patrick stood on a hill waving his staff to drive the snakes of Ireland into the sea.

The shamrock is Patrick's symbol but not the symbol of Ireland.

Patrick is said to have used the three-leaf shamrock in his preaching, probably to explain the doctrine of the Holy Trinity. The Republic of Ireland has a harp as its national symbol.

What about the Saint Patrick's Day celebrations in America?

Well, they began in the later 1700s in Boston, New York, and Philadelphia. Over the next century the celebration spread across the new nation. By 1900, Saint Patrick's Day parades became demonstrations of Irish Catholic pride and, later, of social and political power.

Saint Patrick's prayer was not created by him...but it could have been.

The Lorica of Saint Patrick is a prayer hymn attributed to Patrick. And it has the feel of traditional Irish blessings and prayers. But modern experts date it from the 700s. It is a prayer for protection—the word *lorica* means breastplate.

A lovely tradition has it that the prayer shielded Patrick and his companions from ambush by a chieftain's soldiers. Afterwards Patrick's group approached the chieftain chanting, "Let them that will, trust in chariots and horses, but we walk in the name of the Lord."

Following are three portions of this prayer, from the Old Irish text.

The Lorica of Saint Patrick

I bind to myself today
The power of Heaven,
The brightness of the Sun,
The whiteness of Snow,
The splendor of Fire,
The speed of Lightning,
The swiftness of the Wind,
The depth of the Sea,
The stability of the Earth,
The firmness of Rocks.

I arise today through
God's Power to pilot me,
God's Might to uphold me,
God's Wisdom to guide me,
God's Eye to look before me,
God's Ear to hear me,
God's Word to speak for me,
God's Hand to guard me,
God's Way to lie before me,
God's Shield to shelter me,
God's Host to secure me.

Christ protect me today ...
Christ with me,
Christ before me,
Christ behind me,
Christ in me, Christ beneath me,
Christ above me,
Christ at my right, Christ at my left,
Christ when lying down,
Christ in sitting, Christ in rising up.
Christ in the heart of everyone
who thinks of me,
Christ in the mouth of everyone
who speaks of me,
Christ in every eye that sees me,
Christ in every ear that hears me.

49112800R00027

Made in the USA
Middletown, DE
05 October 2017